JOHN COLTRANE

Play-Along

Recorded by Ric Probst at Tanner Monagle Studio
Trumpet: Jamie Breiwick
Tenor Sax: Jonathan Greenstein
Piano: Mark Davis
Bass: Jeff Hamann
Drums: David Bayles

To access online content, visit:
www.halleonard.com/mylibrary

Enter Code
6505-0537-9810-8212

Cover photo by Wolfgang Kunz/ullstein bild via Getty Images

ISBN 978-1-5400-2636-1

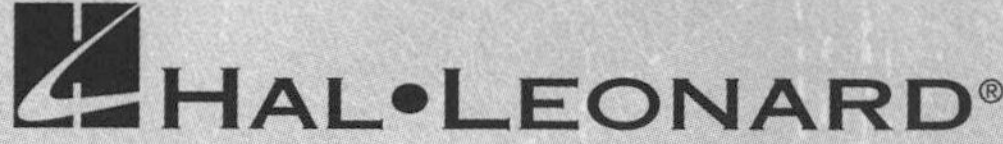

For more information on the Real Book series, including community forums, please visit
www.OfficialRealBook.com

Visit Hal Leonard Online at
www.halleonard.com

Contact Us:
Hal Leonard
7777 West Bluemound Road
Milwaukee, WI 53213
Email: info@halleonard.com

In Europe contact:
Hal Leonard Europe Limited
42 Wigmore Street
Marylebone, London, W1U 2RN
Email: info@halleonardeurope.com

In Australia contact:
Hal Leonard Australia Pty. Ltd.
4 Lentara Court
Cheltenham, Victoria, 3192 Australia
Email: info@halleonard.com.au

Contents

BLUE TRAIN
(BLUE TRANE)

CENTRAL PARK WEST

COUSIN MARY

(UP)

C VERSION

- JOHN COLTRANE

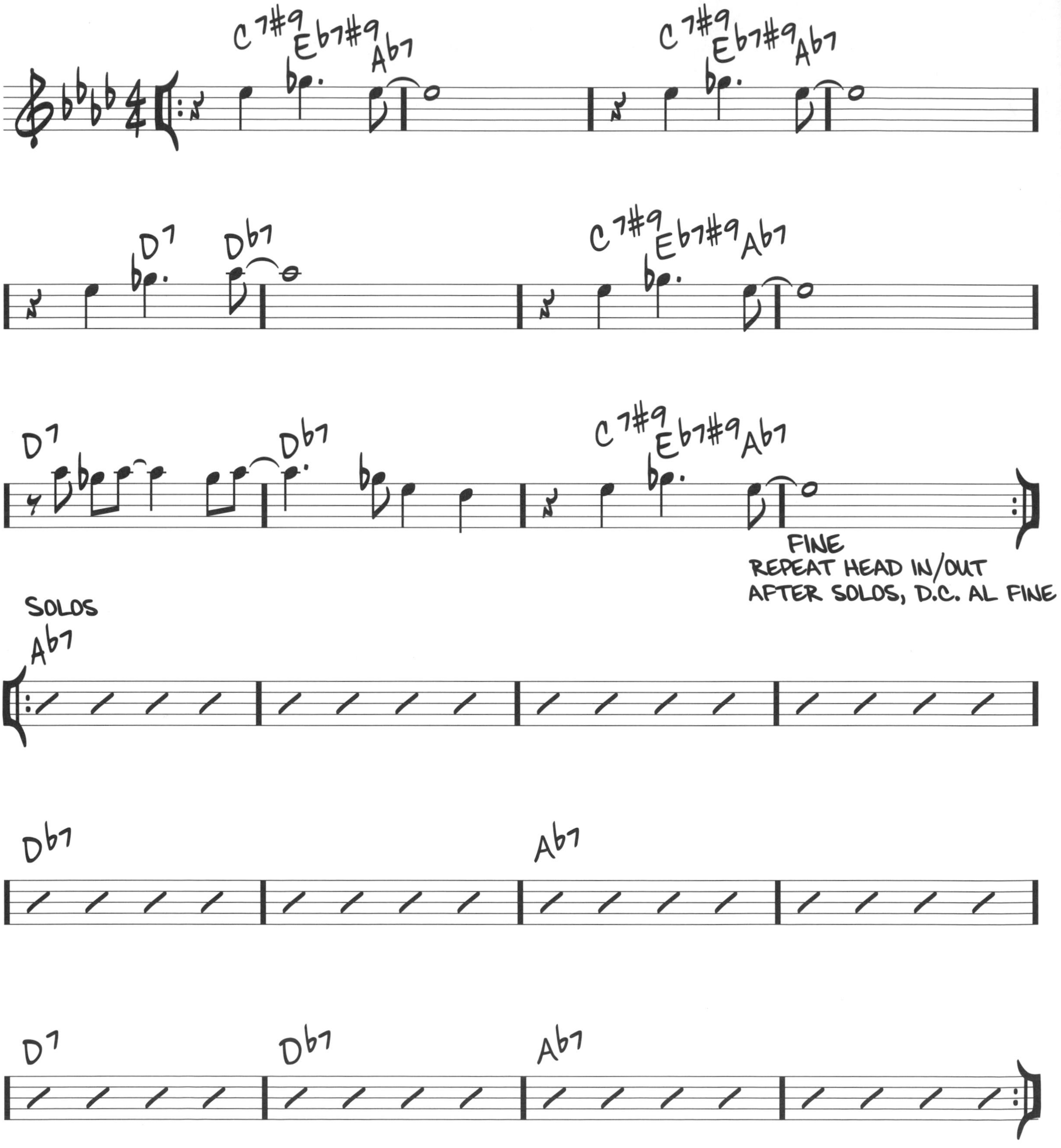

C7#9 Eb7#9 Ab7 C7#9 Eb7#9 Ab7

D7 Db7 C7#9 Eb7#9 Ab7

D7 Db7 C7#9 Eb7#9 Ab7

FINE
REPEAT HEAD IN/OUT
AFTER SOLOS, D.C. AL FINE

SOLOS

Ab7

Db7 Ab7

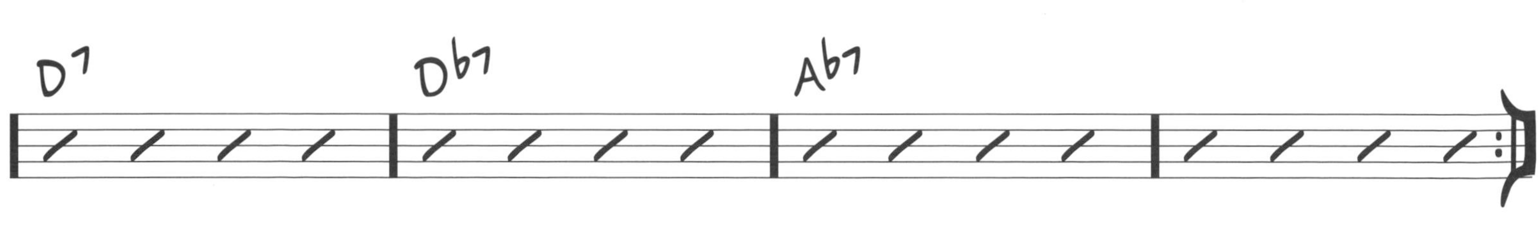

GIANT STEPS
(UP)
C VERSION
- JOHN COLTRANE
Bmaj7 D7 Gmaj7 Bb7 Ebmaj7 A-7 D7
Gmaj7 Bb7 Ebmaj7 F#7 Bmaj7 F-7 Bb7
Ebmaj7 A-7 D7 Gmaj7 C#-7 F#7
Bmaj7 F-7 Bb7 Ebmaj7 1. C#-7 F#7
FINE
2. C#-7 F#7
REPEAT HEAD IN/OUT
AFTER SOLOS, D.C. AL FINE

IMPRESSIONS
(UP)
C VERSION
- JOHN COLTRANE
D-7
Eb-7
D-7
FINE
AFTER SOLOS, D.C. AL FINE
(TAKE REPEAT)

(FAST)
LAZY BIRD
C VERSION
- JOHN COLTRANE
A-7 D7 C-7 F7 F-7 Bb7
Ebmaj7 A-7 D7 Gmaj7 1. Ab-7 Db7 2. A-7 Bb-7
B-7 E7 Amaj7 Bb-7 Eb7
A-7 D7 Gmaj7 Ab-7 Db7
A-7 D7 C-7 F7 F-7 Bb7
Ebmaj7 A-7 D7 TO ⊕ Gmaj7 B-7 Bb7
AFTER SOLOS, D.C. AL ⊕
B-7 E7b9 A-7 D7b9
Gmaj7 C7b9 Fmaj7 Bb7b9
A7b9 Abmaj7 Db9#11

MOMENT'S NOTICE
(UP)
C VERSION
- JOHN COLTRANE
A INTRO
E-7 A7 F-7 Bb7 Ebmaj7 Ab-7 Db7
D-7 G7 Eb-7 Ab7 Dbmaj7 D-7 G7
C-7 Bb-7 Eb7 Abmaj7 Db7
G-7 C-7 F-7 Bb7 Eb/Bb F-/Bb
G-/Bb F-/Bb Eb/Bb F-/Bb G-/Bb F-/Bb Eb N.C.
(FILL - - - - - - - - - - -)
B
*(E-7 A7 F-7 Bb7)
E-7 A7 F-7 Bb7 Ebmaj7 D-7 Db7
*(D-7 G7 Eb-7 Ab7)
D-7 G7 Eb-7 Ab7 Dbmaj7 D-7 G7
* FOR SOLOS
C-7 Bb-7 Eb7 Abmaj7 Db7
1. G-7 C7 Ab-7 Db7 Gbmaj7 F-7 Bb7

2.

G–7 C7 F–7 B♭7 E♭/B♭ F–/B♭

G–/B♭ F–/B♭ E♭/B♭ F–/B♭ G–/B♭ F–/B♭ TO ⊕

E♭ (SOLO BREAK)

SOLOS ON [B] (TAKE REPEAT)
AFTER SOLOS, D.S. AL ⊕
(TAKE REPEAT)

⊕

E♭7♯9

MY FAVORITE THINGS

(FAST)

C VERSION

- OSCAR HAMMERSTEIN II/RICHARD RODGERS

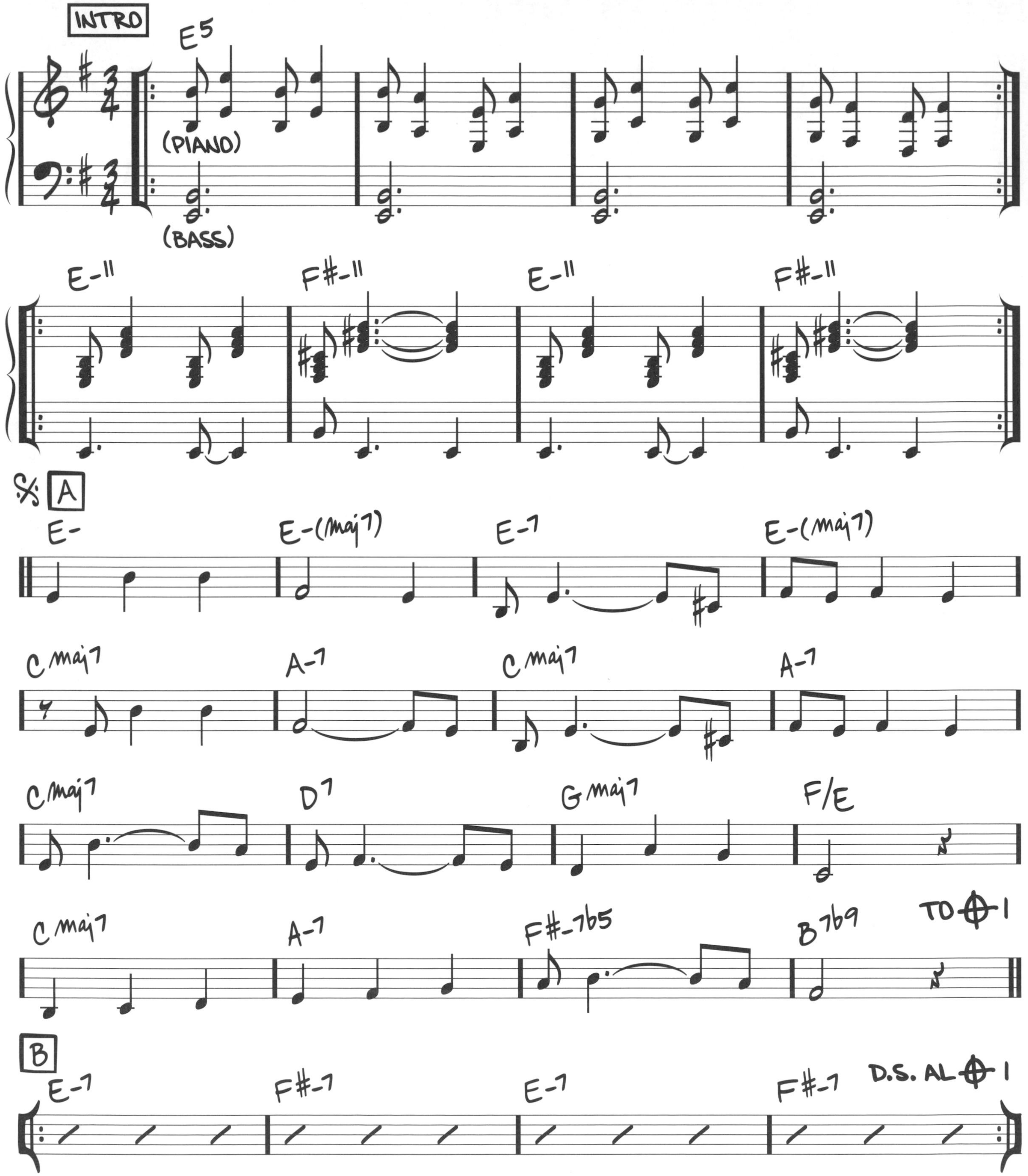
INTRO
E5
(PIANO)
(BASS)
E-11
F#-11
E-11
F#-11
A
E-
E-(maj7)
E-7
E-(maj7)
Cmaj7
A-7
Cmaj7
A-7
Cmaj7
D7
Gmaj7
F/E
Cmaj7
A-7
F#-7b5
B7b9
TO ⊕ 1
B
E-7
F#-7
E-7
F#-7
D.S. AL ⊕ 1

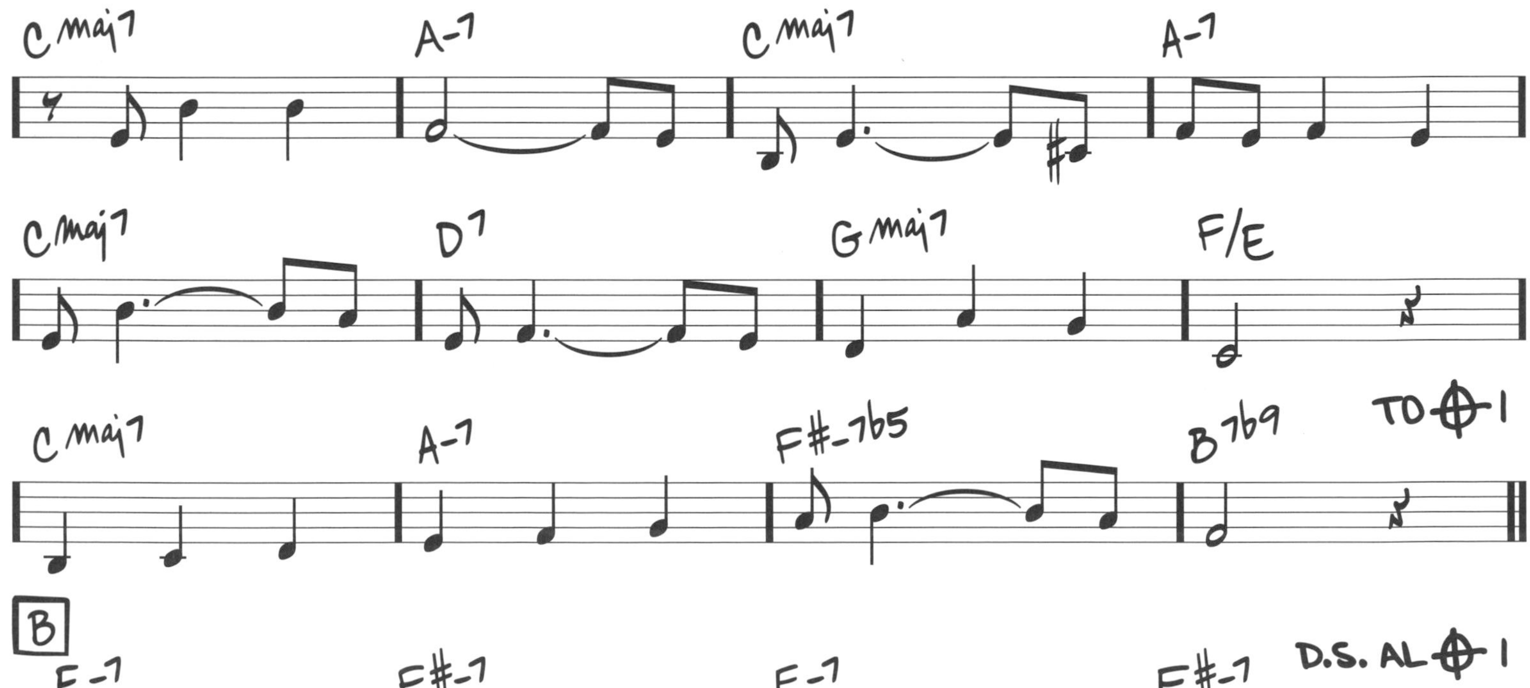

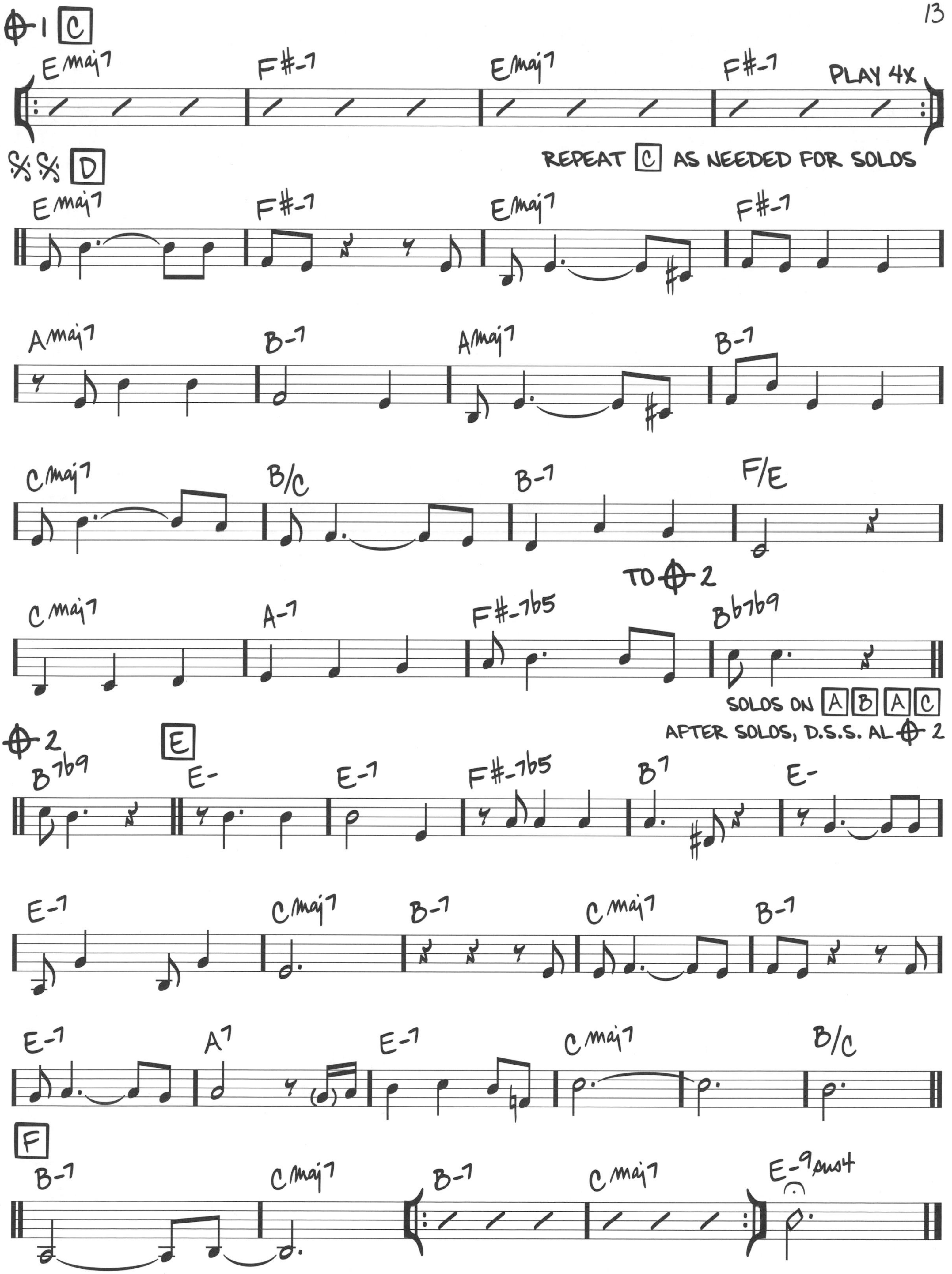

𝄌 1 [C]

Emaj7 | F#-7 | Emaj7 | F#-7

PLAY 4X

REPEAT [C] AS NEEDED FOR SOLOS

𝄋𝄋 [D]

Emaj7 | F#-7 | Emaj7 | F#-7

Amaj7 | B-7 | Amaj7 | B-7

Cmaj7 | B/C | B-7 | F/E

TO 𝄌 2

Cmaj7 | A-7 | F#-7♭5 | B♭7♭9

SOLOS ON [A] [B] [A] [C]

AFTER SOLOS, D.S.S. AL 𝄌 2

𝄌 2

B7♭9

[E]

E- | E-7 | F#-7♭5 | B7 | E-

E-7 | Cmaj7 | B-7 | Cmaj7 | B-7

E-7 | A7 | E-7 | Cmaj7 | B/C

[F]

B-7 | Cmaj7 | B-7 | Cmaj7 | E-9sus4

SYEEDA'S SONG FLUTE

FINE
SOLOS
G
Ab7
G
Ab7
G
Ab7
G
F#7
G-
Abmaj7
G-
Abmaj7
G-
Abmaj7
G-
Abmaj7
G
Ab7
G
Ab7
G
Ab7
G
F#7
E7
D7
E7
F#7
AFTER SOLOS, D.S. AL FINE

NAIMA
(NIEMA)
(BALLAD)
C VERSION
- JOHN COLTRANE
TO ⊕
AFTER SOLOS, D.S. AL ⊕

(MED. SWING)
BLUE TRAIN
(BLUE TRANE)
- JOHN COLTRANE
B♭ VERSION
F7#9
B♭7#11
F7#9
C7#9
1.
F7#9
2.
F7#9
FINE
AFTER SOLOS, D.S. AL FINE
(PLAY PICKUPS) (TAKE REPEAT)
SOLOS
F7
B♭7
F7
B♭7
F7
D7
G-7
C7
F7
G-7
C7

(BALLAD)
CENTRAL PARK WEST
Bb VERSION
- JOHN COLTRANE
Eb-7 Ab7
Dbmaj7 Gb-7 Cb7
Fbmaj7 C-7 F7
Bbmaj7 A-7 D7
Gmaj7 Eb-7 Ab7
Dbmaj7 Gb-7 Cb7
Fbmaj7 Eb-7 Ab7
Dbmaj7
LAST X, TO
Eb-7/Db
Dbmaj7
1.
Eb-7/Db Eb-7 Ab7
2.
Eb-7/Db Eb-7 Ab7
AFTER SOLOS, D.S. AL
(PLAY PICKUPS) (TAKE REPEAT)
Eb-7/Db Eb-7 Ab7
Dbmaj7

COUSIN MARY
(UP)
B♭ VERSION
- JOHN COLTRANE
D7#9
F7#9
B♭7
E7
E♭7
FINE
REPEAT HEAD IN/OUT
AFTER SOLOS, D.C. AL FINE
SOLOS

GIANT STEPS

(UP)
Bb VERSION
- JOHN COLTRANE
C#maj7 E7 Amaj7 C7 Fmaj7 B-7 E7
Amaj7 C7 Fmaj7 Ab7 Dbmaj7 G-7 C7
Fmaj7 B-7 E7 Amaj7 Eb-7 Ab7
Dbmaj7 Ab G-7 C7 Fmaj7 1. Eb-7 Ab7
FINE
2. Eb-7 Ab7
REPEAT HEAD IN/OUT
AFTER SOLOS, D.C. AL FINE

IMPRESSIONS

(FAST)
LAZY BIRD
B♭ VERSION
- JOHN COLTRANE
B-7 E7 D-7 G7 G-7 C7
Fmaj7 B-7 E7 Amaj7 1. B♭-7 E♭7 2. B-7 C-7
C#-7 F#7 Bmaj7 C-7 F7
3 3
B-7 E7 Amaj7 B♭-7 E♭7
3 3
B-7 E7 D-7 G7 G-7 C7
Fmaj7 B-7 E7 TO ⊕ Amaj7 C#-7 C7
AFTER SOLOS, D.C. AL ⊕
⊕ C#-7 F#7♭9 B-7 E7♭9
Amaj7 D7♭9 Gmaj7 C7♭9
B7♭9 B♭maj7 E♭9#11

NAIMA
(NIEMA)
(BALLAD)
- JOHN COLTRANE
B♭ VERSION
C-7/F F-7 Bmaj7#11/F Amaj7#11/F B♭maj7/F
D♭maj7/C C13♭9 D♭maj7/C C13♭9
D♭-9(maj7)/C D♭maj7/C G-9/C A♭13/F
C-7/F F-7 Bmaj7#11/F Amaj7#11/F B♭maj7/F
TO ⊕
AFTER SOLOS, D.S. AL ⊕
B♭maj7/F Bmaj7#11/F Amaj7#11/F B♭maj7/F Bmaj7#11/F Amaj7#11/F
B♭maj7 E♭maj7 B♭maj7 E♭maj7 B♭maj7 E♭maj7 B♭maj7

MOMENT'S NOTICE
(UP)
Bb VERSION
- JOHN COLTRANE
A
INTRO
F#-7 B7 G-7 C7 Fmaj7 Bb-7 Eb7
E-7 A7 F-7 Bb7 Ebmaj7 E-7 A7
D-7 C-7 F7 Bbmaj7 Eb7
A-7 D-7 G-7 C7 F/C G-/C
A-/C G-/C F/C G-/C A-/C G-/C F N.C.
(FILL - - - - - - - - - - - - -)
B
*(F#-7 B7 G-7 C7)
F#-7 B7 G-7 C7 Fmaj7 E-7 Eb7
*(E-7 A7 F-7 Bb7)
E-7 A7 F-7 Bb7 Ebmaj7 E-7 A7
* FOR SOLOS
D-7 C-7 F7 Bbmaj7 Eb7
1.
A-7 D7 Bb-7 Eb7 Abmaj7 G-7 C7

2.

A-7 D7 G-7 C7 F/C G-/C

A-/C G-/C F/C G-/C A-/C G-/C TO ⊕

F (SOLO BREAK)

SOLOS ON B (TAKE REPEAT)
AFTER SOLOS, D.S. AL ⊕
(TAKE REPEAT)

⊕

F7♯9

MY FAVORITE THINGS

(FAST)

B♭ VERSION

- OSCAR HAMMERSTEIN II/RICHARD RODGERS

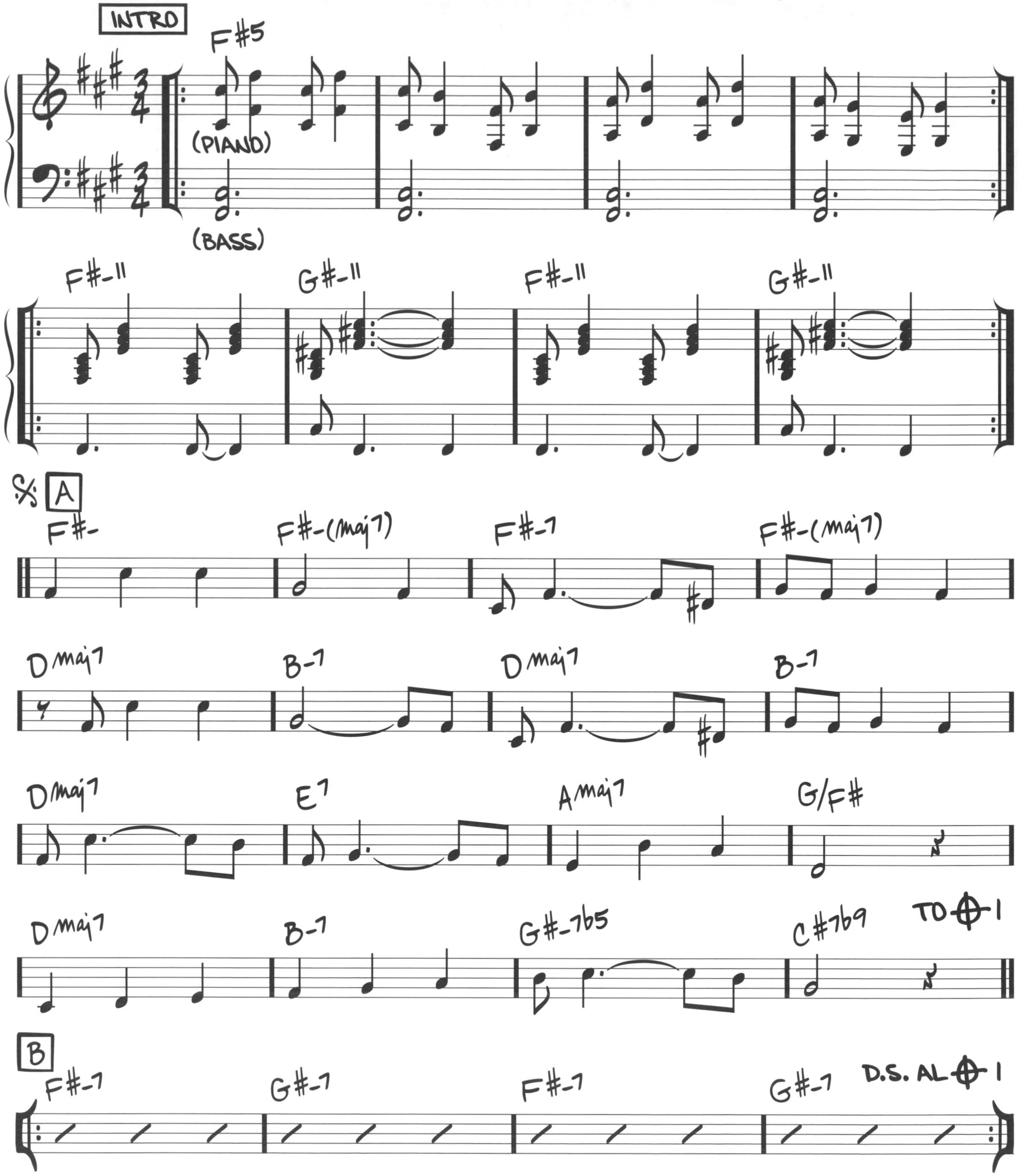

INTRO

F#5

(PIANO)

(BASS)

F#-11 G#-11 F#-11 G#-11

A

F#- F#-(maj7) F#-7 F#-(maj7)

Dmaj7 B-7 Dmaj7 B-7

Dmaj7 E7 Amaj7 G/F#

Dmaj7 B-7 G#-7♭5 C#7♭9 TO ⊕ 1

B

F#-7 G#-7 F#-7 G#-7 D.S. AL ⊕ 1

Coda 1 C

F#maj7 | G#-7 | F#maj7 | G#-7 PLAY 4X

REPEAT C AS NEEDED FOR SOLOS

Segno Segno D

F#maj7 | G#-7 | F#maj7 | G#-7

Bmaj7 | C#-7 | Bmaj7 | C#-7

Dmaj7 | C#/D | C#-7 | G/F#

TO Coda 2

Dmaj7 | B-7 | G#-7b5 | C7b9

SOLOS ON A B A C

AFTER SOLOS, D.S.S. AL Coda 2

Coda 2

C#7b9

E

F#- | F#-7 | G#-7b5 | C#7 | F#-

F#-7 | Dmaj7 | C#-7 | Dmaj7 | C#-7

F#-7 | B7 | F#-7 | Dmaj7 | C#/D

F

C#-7 | Dmaj7 | C#-7 | Dmaj7 | F#-9sus4

SYEEDA'S SONG FLUTE
(MED.)
Bb VERSION
- JOHN COLTRANE
INTRO
N.C.
(BASS & PIANO)
1.
2.
W/INTRO RIFF
N.C.
A-
Bbmaj7
A-
Bbmaj7
A-
Bbmaj7
E7#9
A-
B-7
Bb7
W/INTRO RIFF
N.C.
8VB (OPTIONAL)
(BS. & PNO. 8VB)

8VB (OPTIONAL)
FINE
SOLOS
A
Bb7
A
Bb7
A
Bb7
A
G#7
A-
Bbmaj7
A-
Bbmaj7
A-
Bbmaj7
A-
Bbmaj7
A
Bb7
A
Bb7
A
Bb7
A
G#7
F#7
E7
F#7
G#7
AFTER SOLOS, D.S. AL FINE

BLUE TRAIN
(BLUE TRANE)
(MED. SWING)
E♭ VERSION
- JOHN COLTRANE
C7#9
F7#11
C7#9
G7#9
1. C7#9
2. C7#9
FINE
AFTER SOLOS, D.S. AL FINE
(PLAY PICKUPS) (TAKE REPEAT)
SOLOS
C7
F7
C7
F7
C7
A7
D-7
G7
C7
D-7
G7

(BALLAD)
CENTRAL PARK WEST
Eb VERSION
- JOHN COLTRANE
Bb-7 Eb7 Abmaj7 Db-7 Gb7 Cbmaj7 G-7 C7 Fmaj7 E-7 Ab7
Dmaj7 Bb-7 Eb7 Abmaj7 Db-7 Gb7 Cbmaj7 Bb-7 Eb7 Abmaj7
Bb-7/Ab Abmaj7 Bb-7/Ab Bb-7 Eb7 Bb-7/Ab Bb-7 Eb7
LAST X, TO
AFTER SOLOS, D.S. AL
(PLAY PICKUPS) (TAKE REPEAT)
Bb-7/Ab Bb-7 Eb7 Abmaj7

COUSIN MARY

(UP)

E♭ VERSION

– JOHN COLTRANE

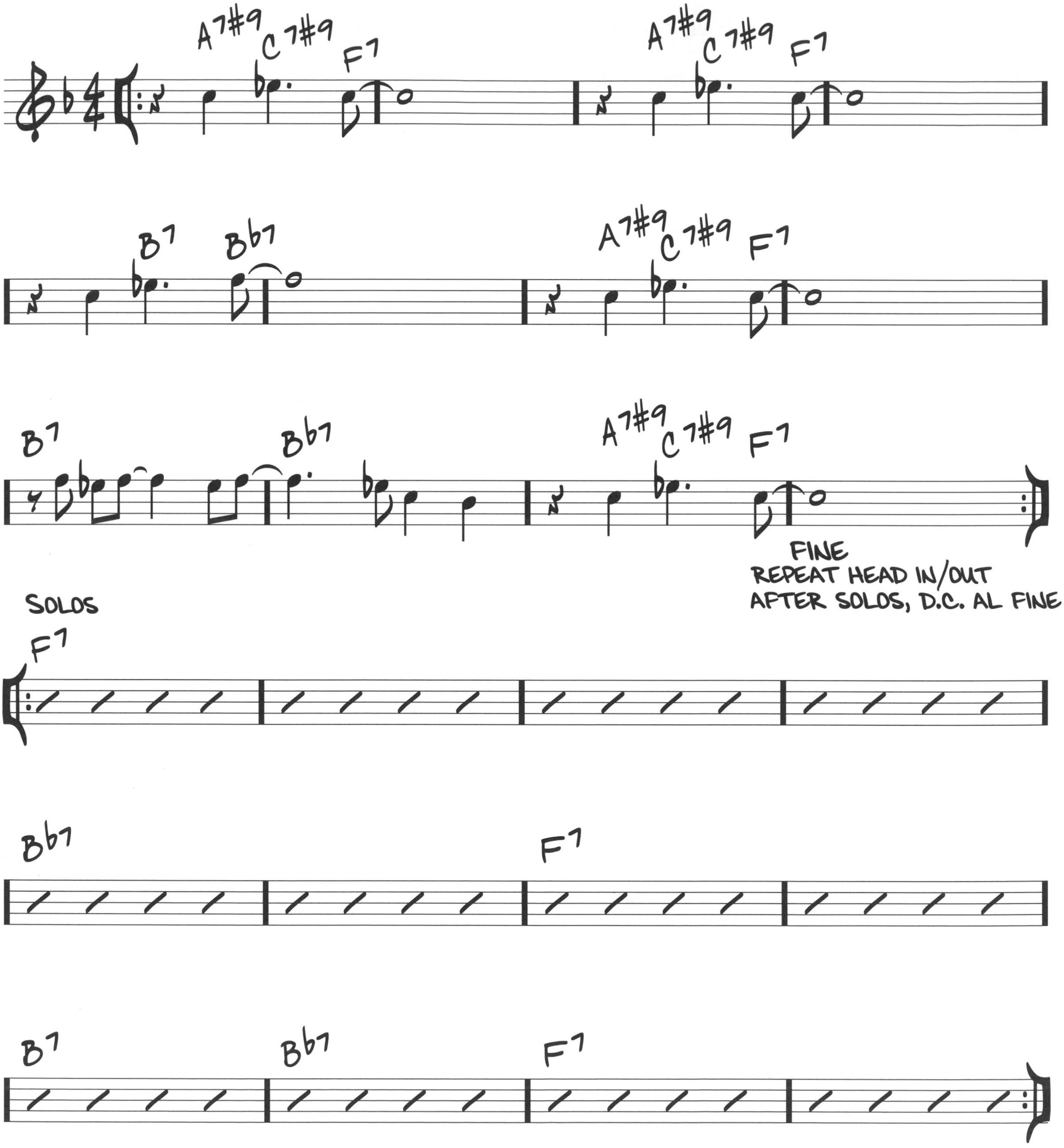

A7#9 C7#9 F7 A7#9 C7#9 F7

B7 B♭7 A7#9 C7#9 F7

B7 B♭7 A7#9 C7#9 F7

FINE
REPEAT HEAD IN/OUT
AFTER SOLOS, D.C. AL FINE

SOLOS

F7

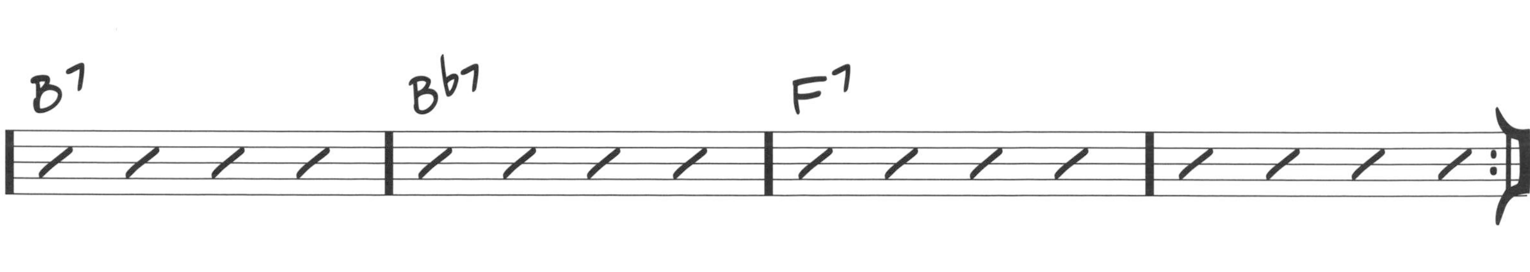

GIANT STEPS
(UP)
E♭ VERSION
- JOHN COLTRANE
G#maj7 B7 Emaj7 G7 Cmaj7 F#-7 B7
Emaj7 G7 Cmaj7 Eb7 Abmaj7 D-7 G7
Cmaj7 F#-7 B7 Emaj7 Bb-7 Eb7
Abmaj7 D-7 G7 Cmaj7 1. Bb-7 Eb7
FINE
2. Bb-7 Eb7
REPEAT HEAD IN/OUT
AFTER SOLOS, D.C. AL FINE

IMPRESSIONS

(FAST)
LAZY BIRD
Eb VERSION
- JOHN COLTRANE
F#-7 B7 A-7 D7 D-7 G7
CMAJ7 F#-7 B7 EMAJ7 F-7 Bb7 F#-7 G-7
G#-7 C#7 F#MAJ7 G-7 C7
F#-7 B7 EMAJ7 F-7 Bb7
F#-7 B7 A-7 D7 D-7 G7
CMAJ7 F#-7 B7 TO EMAJ7 G#-7 G7
AFTER SOLOS, D.C. AL
G#-7 C#7b9 F#-7 B7b9
EMAJ7 A7b9 DMAJ7 G7b9
F#7b9 FMAJ7 Bb9#11

MOMENT'S NOTICE

2.

E-7 A7 | D-7 G7 | C/G | D-/G |

E-/G | D-/G | C/G D-/G | E-/G D-/G

TO 𝄌

C (SOLO BREAK)

SOLOS ON B (TAKE REPEAT)
AFTER SOLOS, D.S. AL 𝄌
(TAKE REPEAT)

𝄌

C7#9

MY FAVORITE THINGS

(FAST)
E♭ VERSION

- OSCAR HAMMERSTEIN II/RICHARD RODGERS

Φ 1 C

C#maj7 | D#-7 | C#maj7 | D#-7 PLAY 4X

𝄋𝄋 D

REPEAT C AS NEEDED FOR SOLOS

C#maj7 | D#-7 | C#maj7 | D#-7

F#maj7 | G#-7 | F#maj7 | G#-7

Amaj7 | G#/A | G#-7 | D/C#

Amaj7 | F#-7 | D#-7b5 | TO Φ 2 G7b9

SOLOS ON A B A C

AFTER SOLOS, D.S.S. AL Φ 2

Φ 2

G#7b9 | E C#- | C#-7 | D#-7b5 | G#7 | C#-

C#-7 | Amaj7 | G#-7 | Amaj7 | G#-7

C#-7 | F#7 | C#-7 | Amaj7 | | G#/A

F

G#-7 | Amaj7 | G#-7 | Amaj7 | C#-9sus4

(MED.)
SYEEDA'S SONG FLUTE
E♭ VERSION
- JOHN COLTRANE
INTRO
N.C.
1.
2.
(BASS & PIANO)
W/INTRO RIFF
N.C.
E-
FMAJ7
E-
FMAJ7
E-
FMAJ7
B7#9
E-
F#-7
F7
W/INTRO RIFF
N.C.
(BS. & PNO. 8VB)

AFTER SOLOS, D.S. AL FINE

NAIMA
(NIEMA)
(BALLAD)
Eb VERSION
- JOHN COLTRANE
G-7/C
C-7
Gbmaj7#11/C
Emaj7#11/C
Fmaj7/C
Abmaj7/G
G13b9
Abmaj7/G
G13b9
Ab-9(maj7)/G
Abmaj7/G
D-9/G
Eb13/C
TO
G-7/C
C-7
Gbmaj7#11/C
Emaj7#11/C
Fmaj7/C
AFTER SOLOS, D.S. AL
Fmaj7/C
Gbmaj7#11/C
Emaj7#11/C
Fmaj7/C
Gbmaj7#11/C
Emaj7#11/C
Fmaj7
Bbmaj7
Fmaj7
Bbmaj7
Fmaj7
Bbmaj7
Fmaj7

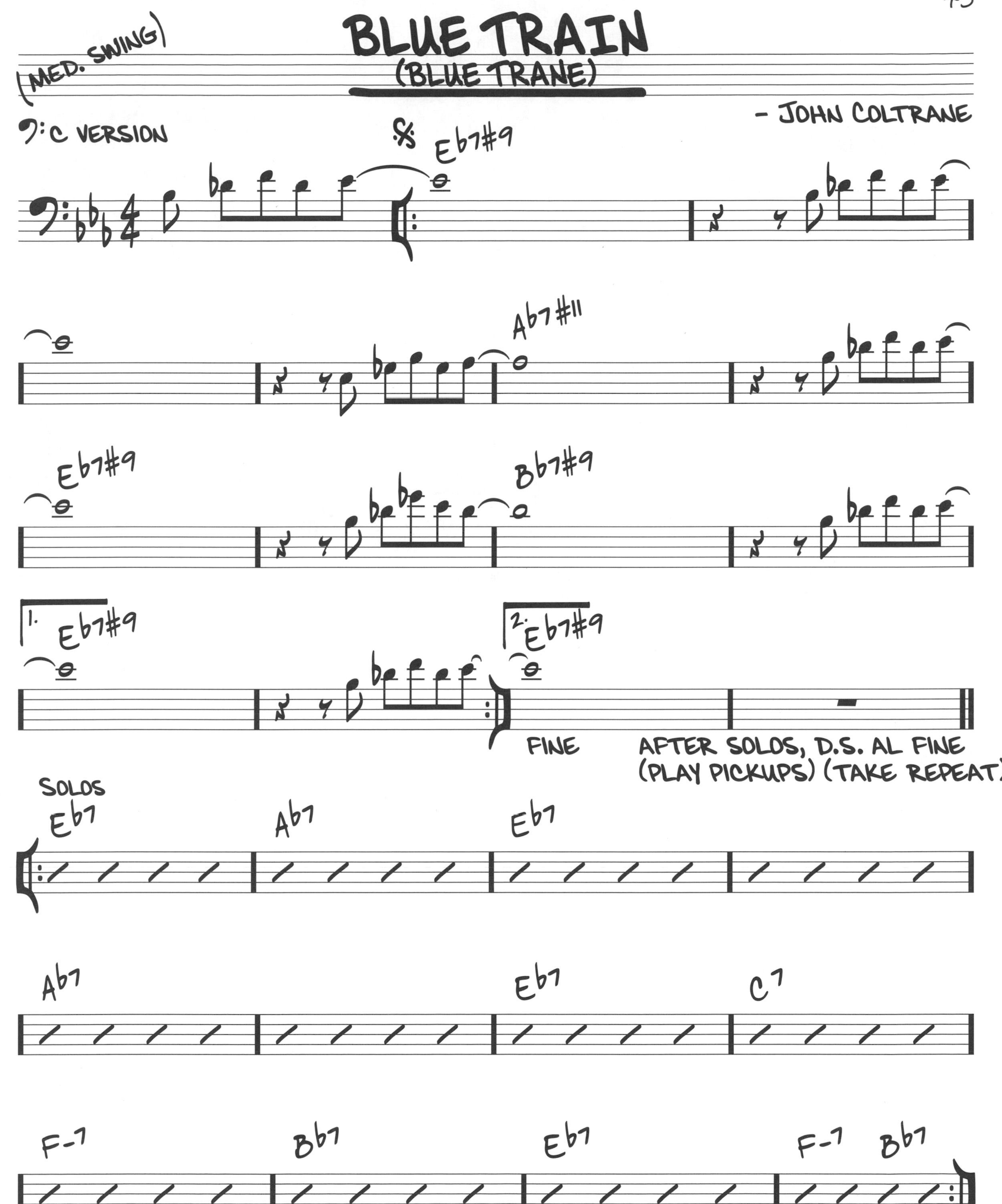
BLUE TRAIN
(BLUE TRANE)
(MED. SWING)
- JOHN COLTRANE
C VERSION
Eb7#9
Ab7#11
Eb7#9
Bb7#9
1. Eb7#9
2. Eb7#9
FINE
AFTER SOLOS, D.S. AL FINE
(PLAY PICKUPS) (TAKE REPEAT)
SOLOS
Eb7
Ab7
Eb7
Ab7
Eb7
C7
F-7
Bb7
Eb7
F-7
Bb7

CENTRAL PARK WEST

COUSIN MARY

(UP)

- JOHN COLTRANE

GIANT STEPS
(UP)
C VERSION
- JOHN COLTRANE
Bmaj7 D7 Gmaj7 Bb7 Ebmaj7 A-7 D7
Gmaj7 Bb7 Ebmaj7 F#7 Bmaj7 F-7 Bb7
Ebmaj7 A-7 D7 Gmaj7 C#-7 F#7
Bmaj7 F-7 Bb7 Ebmaj7 1. C#-7 F#7
FINE
2. C#-7 F#7
REPEAT HEAD IN/OUT
AFTER SOLOS, D.C. AL FINE

IMPRESSIONS

(FAST)
LAZY BIRD
C VERSION
- JOHN COLTRANE
A-7 D7 C-7 F7 F-7 Bb7
Ebmaj7 A-7 D7 Gmaj7 Ab-7 Db7 A-7 Bb-7
B-7 E7 Amaj7 Bb-7 Eb7
A-7 D7 Gmaj7 Ab-7 Db7
A-7 D7 C-7 F7 F-7 Bb7
Ebmaj7 A-7 D7 TO Gmaj7 B-7 Bb7
AFTER SOLOS, D.C. AL
B-7 E7b9 A-7 D7b9
Gmaj7 C7b9 Fmaj7 Bb7b9
A7b9 Abmaj7 Db9#11

NAIMA
(NIEMA)
(BALLAD)
- JOHN COLTRANE
C VERSION
Bb-7/Eb Eb-7 Amaj7#11/Eb Gmaj7#11/Eb Abmaj7/Eb
Bmaj7/Bb Bb13b9 Bmaj7/Bb Bb13b9
B-9(maj7)/Bb Bmaj7/Bb F-9/Bb Gb13/Eb
TO ⊕
Bb-7/Eb Eb-7 Amaj7#11/Eb Gmaj7#11/Eb Abmaj7/Eb
AFTER SOLOS, D.S. AL ⊕
Abmaj7/Eb Amaj7#11/Eb Gmaj7#11/Eb Abmaj7/Eb Amaj7#11/Eb Gmaj7#11/Eb
Abmaj7 Dbmaj7 Abmaj7 Dbmaj7 Abmaj7 Dbmaj7 Abmaj7

MOMENT'S NOTICE
(UP)
C VERSION
- JOHN COLTRANE
A INTRO
E-7 A7 F-7 Bb7 Ebmaj7 Ab-7 Db7
D-7 G7 Eb-7 Ab7 Dbmaj7 D-7 G7
C-7 Bb-7 Eb7 Abmaj7 Db7
G-7 C-7 F-7 Bb7 Eb/Bb F-/Bb
G-/Bb F-/Bb Eb/Bb F-/Bb G-/Bb F-/Bb Eb N.C.
(FILL - - - - - - - - - - - -)
B
*(E-7 A7 F-7 Bb7)
E-7 A7 F-7 Bb7 Ebmaj7 D-7 Db7
*(D-7 G7 Eb-7 Ab7)
D-7 G7 Eb-7 Ab7 Dbmaj7 D-7 G7
* FOR SOLOS
C-7 Bb-7 Eb7 Abmaj7 Db7
1.
G-7 C7 Ab-7 Db7 Gbmaj7 F-7 Bb7

2. G-7 C7 F-7 Bb7 Eb/Bb F-/Bb

G-/Bb F-/Bb Eb/Bb F-/Bb G-/Bb F-/Bb TO ⊕

Eb (SOLO BREAK)

SOLOS ON [B] (TAKE REPEAT)
AFTER SOLOS, D.S. AL ⊕
(TAKE REPEAT)

⊕ Eb7#9

(FAST)

C VERSION

- OSCAR HAMMERSTEIN II/RICHARD RODGERS

INTRO

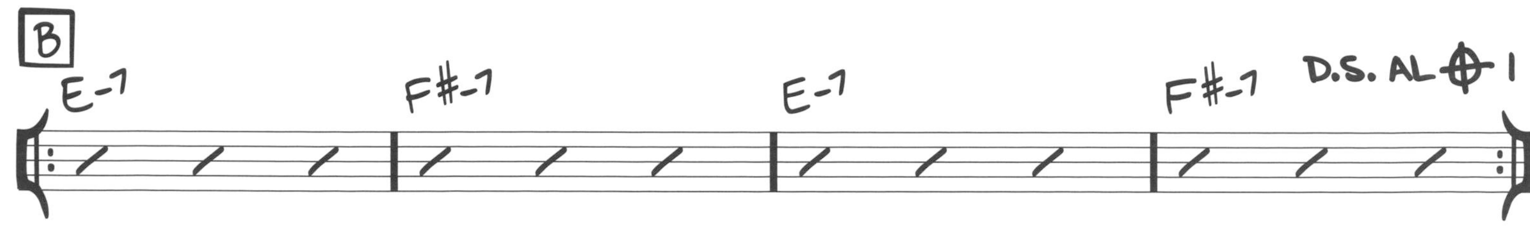

C

Emaj7 F#-7 Emaj7 F#-7

PLAY 4X

D

REPEAT C AS NEEDED FOR SOLOS

Emaj7 F#-7 Emaj7 F#-7

Amaj7 B-7 Amaj7 B-7

Cmaj7 B/C B-7 F/E

TO 2

Cmaj7 A-7 F#-7b5 Bb7b9

SOLOS ON A B A C

AFTER SOLOS, D.S.S. AL 2

E

B7b9 E- E-7 F#-7b5 B7 E-

E-7 Cmaj7 B-7 Cmaj7 B-7

E-7 A7 E-7 Cmaj7 B/C

F

B-7 Cmaj7 B-7 Cmaj7 E-9sus4

SYEEDA'S SONG FLUTE
(MED.)
C VERSION
- JOHN COLTRANE
INTRO
N.C.
(BASS & PIANO)
W/INTRO RIFF
N.C.
G-
Abmaj7
D7#9
A-7
Ab7
W/INTRO RIFF
N.C.
(BS. & PNO.)

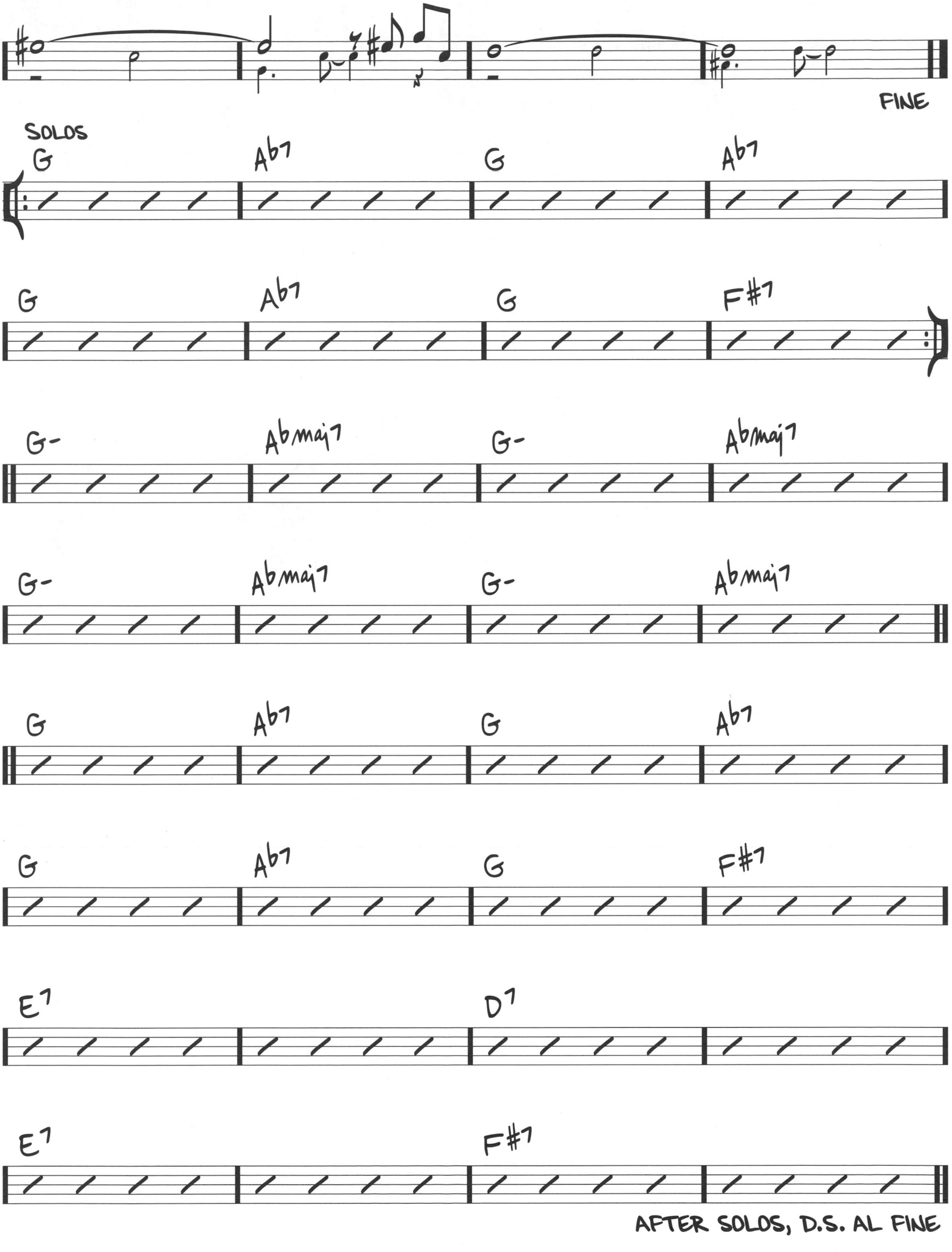

FINE

SOLOS

G | Ab7 | G | Ab7

G | Ab7 | G | F#7

G- | Abmaj7 | G- | Abmaj7

G- | Abmaj7 | G- | Abmaj7

G | Ab7 | G | Ab7

G | Ab7 | G | F#7

E7 | | D7 |

E7 | | F#7 |

AFTER SOLOS, D.S. AL FINE

THE REAL BOOK MULTI-TRACKS

1. MAIDEN VOYAGE PLAY-ALONG

Autumn Leaves • Blue Bossa • Doxy • Footprints • Maiden Voyage • Now's the Time • On Green Dolphin Street • Satin Doll • Summertime • Tune Up.

00196616 Book with Online Media........$17.99

2. MILES DAVIS PLAY-ALONG

Blue in Green • Boplicity (Be Bop Lives) • Four • Freddie Freeloader • Milestones • Nardis • Seven Steps to Heaven • So What • Solar • Walkin'.

00196798 Book with Online Media........$17.99

3. ALL BLUES PLAY-ALONG

All Blues • Back at the Chicken Shack • Billie's Bounce (Bill's Bounce) • Birk's Works • Blues by Five • C-Jam Blues • Mr. P.C. • One for Daddy-O • Reunion Blues • Turnaround.

00196692 Book with Online Media........$17.99

4. CHARLIE PARKER PLAY-ALONG

Anthropology • Blues for Alice • Confirmation • Donna Lee • K.C. Blues • Moose the Mooche • My Little Suede Shoes • Ornithology • Scrapple from the Apple • Yardbird Suite.

00196799 Book with Online Media........$17.99

5. JAZZ FUNK PLAY-ALONG

Alligator Bogaloo • The Chicken • Cissy Strut • Cold Duck Time • Comin' Home Baby • Mercy, Mercy, Mercy • Put It Where You Want It • Sidewinder • Tom Cat • Watermelon Man.

00196728 Book with Online Media........$17.99

6. SONNY ROLLINS PLAY-ALONG

Airegin • Blue Seven • Doxy • Duke of Iron • Oleo • Pent up House • St. Thomas • Sonnymoon for Two • Strode Rode • Tenor Madness.

00218264 Book with Online Media........$17.99

7. THELONIOUS MONK PLAY-ALONG

Bemsha Swing • Blue Monk • Bright Mississippi • Green Chimneys • Monk's Dream • Reflections • Rhythm-a-ning • 'Round Midnight • Straight No Chaser • Ugly Beauty.

00232768 Book with Online Media........$17.99

8. BEBOP ERA PLAY-ALONG

Au Privave • Boneology • Bouncing with Bud • Dexterity • Groovin' High • Half Nelson • In Walked Bud • Lady Bird • Move • Witches Pit.

00196728 Book with Online Media........$17.99

9. CHRISTMAS CLASSICS PLAY-ALONG

Blue Christmas • Christmas Time Is Here • Frosty the Snow Man • Have Yourself a Merry Little Christmas • I'll Be Home for Christmas • My Favorite Things • Santa Claus Is Comin' to Town • Silver Bells • White Christmas • Winter Wonderland.

00236808 Book with Online Media........$17.99

10. CHRISTMAS SONGS PLAY-ALONG

Away in a Manger • The First Noel • Go, Tell It on the Mountain • Hark! the Herald Angels Sing • Jingle Bells • Joy to the World • O Come, All Ye Faithful • O Holy Night • Up on the Housetop • We Wish You a Merry Christmas.

00236809 Book with Online Media........$17.99

15. CHRISTMAS TUNES PLAY-ALONG

The Christmas Song (Chestnuts Roasting on an Open Fire) • Do You Hear What I Hear • Feliz Navidad • Here Comes Santa Claus (Right down Santa Claus Lane) • A Holly Jolly Christmas • Let It Snow! Let It Snow! Let It Snow! • The Little Drummer Boy • The Most Wonderful Time of the Year • Rudolph the Red-Nosed Reindeer • Sleigh Ride.

00278073 Book with Online Media........$17.99

www.halleonard.com

Prices, content and availability subject to change without notice.

0718
333